Boost Your Child's Self-Esteem

Berkley titles by Karin Ireland

150 WAYS TO HELP YOUR CHILD SUCCEED
BOOST YOUR CHILD'S SELF-ESTEEM

Boost Your Child's Self-Esteem

SIMPLE, EFFECTIVE WAYS TO
BUILD CHILDREN'S SELF-RESPECT
AND CONFIDENCE

Karin Ireland

BERKLEY BOOKS, NEW YORK

This book is an original publication of The Berkley Publishing Group.

BOOST YOUR CHILD'S SELF-ESTEEM

A Berkley Book / published by arrangement with the author

PRINTING HISTORY
Berkley trade paperback edition / April 2000

The Penguin Putnam Inc. World Wide Web site address is
http://www.penguinputnam.com

ISBN: 0-425-17295-3

BERKLEY®
Berkley Books are published by The Berkley Publishing Group,
a division of Penguin Putnam Inc.,
375 Hudson Street, New York, New York 10014.
BERKLEY and the "B" design
are trademarks belonging to Penguin Putnam Inc.

PRINTED IN THE UNITED STATES OF AMERICA

10 9 8 7 6 5 4 3 2 1

*For Tom, for being the best co-parent,
and for Tricia, for being the best kid*

Acknowledgments

Mahalo nui loa to my family and friends, who boost my self-esteem every day. Thanks to each and every parent who has chosen to raise their child with love, compassion and humor, to parent with their heart instead of their ego. And special thanks to Christine Zika and Hillary Cige, both great editors, and to Julie Castiglia, my agent and true friend.

A child with self-esteem is a wonderful sight—full of confidence, enthusiasm and life. A child with self-esteem is comfortable with new people and new situations, he believes he can achieve his goals, he's willing to try and he usually succeeds.

Self-esteem may be the most important factor to determine whether a child is successful now and as an adult.

Schools teach essential skills like reading, writing and arithmetic, they teach helpful skills like cooking, music, art and carpentry and they teach some skills that no one will ever use once they're out of school. But few have programs that help children develop good self-esteem.

This job is left for the parents, and it can be one of the most enjoyable and rewarding jobs you'll ever have. Heartwarming moments guaranteed.

Here are 150 ways to boost your child's self-esteem. They don't take money, they don't take any particular skill and most don't take but a few minutes of your time. They're fun, they bring you and your child closer together and they work!

Find Something Positive to Say to Your Child Every Morning Before School.

What a great way to start off the day! Psychologists tell us that our attitudes create our experiences, and having a great attitude on the way to school is one way to create great experiences.

Look for Ways to Be a Partner with Your Child.

Children love to feel like equals to their parents, and being partners for charity or community events is a way in which everybody wins.

Start a collection bag and when you go to the market, ask him to choose something to add to it. When the box or bag is full, invite him to help you decide whether to take it to the food bank, to a church or to a family you know that needs a little help, and then go there together.

When he's outgrown his toys ask him if he'd like to go with you to take them to a shelter (be sure these are toys he's ready to part with, though).

You could adopt an elderly person and once or twice a month do something around the house that he or she can't manage. While you're busy, your child can read or tell them a story.

Teach Your Child How to Solve Problems.

The first step your child needs to take to solve a problem is to recognize that she has one and that she can solve it. When children are very young their parents take care of every detail and as they get older, they need to be shown that they can begin to solve some problems on their own.

Here are seven problem-solving steps your child should keep in mind:

◙ Identify what the problem is.

◙ Decide what she wants the solution to be.

◙ Determine the steps that need to be taken to reach that solution.

- Decide if she can take the steps alone or if she needs help.

- If she needs help, decide who the person best qualified (not nearest or easiest to ask) is.

- Look for something the person she asks will gain by helping her.

- Ask for the results she wants.

If she has to decide whether to do something or not, show her how to make a "plus" and "minus" scorecard by making two columns and listing all the reasons she should do something in one and all the reasons she shouldn't in the other.

Encourage her to notice the way her body feels when she's solving a problem. The best answers will generally be accompanied by feelings of lightness, completion, peace.

When Correcting Your Child, Speak from Your Heart, Not Your Ego.

E very once in a while put yourself in your child's shoes. Or remember how you felt as a child. Then ask yourself questions like these: Do I correct him without making him feel inadequate? Is this the way I'd like to be treated? Am I remembering to attack the problem and not the child? Am I able to say yes most of the time? When I say no, do I say no kindly, the way I'd want him to say it to me?

When it feels like you're parenting from your ego (you're angry, frustrated), call a time-out. After everybody's calm, look at the situation again and look for ways to parent from your heart.

Don't Finish Your Child's Thoughts for Her.

You're rushed, she's daydreaming while she's talking and so you finish her sentence for her. She doesn't seem to mind and maybe she doesn't, but this approach won't help her learn to formulate clear thoughts on her own.

If it seems like she's pausing because she's gotten distracted, gently bring her back to the subject by repeating her last few words encouragingly. If it seems like she's pausing because she's looking for the right words, try to be patient. The more confident she becomes with expressing her thoughts and beliefs the quicker her thoughts will come.

Look for the Message Behind Your Words.

It's easy to feel exasperated when it doesn't seem like your child is doing something the "right" way and it's easy to sound impatient when you're feeling rushed. You may unknowingly send the message that you disapprove of what she's doing without realizing that it sounds like you disapprove of *him*. Instead of challenging your child to improve, this is more likely to make him feel incompetent and unappreciated. For example:

WHAT YOU SAY	WHAT HE HEARS	TRY THIS, INSTEAD
Don't forget your lunch again.	*You're irresponsible.*	*Do you have your lunch?*
Let me do that for you.	*You're incompetent.*	*That's tricky—do you want help?*

WHAT YOU SAY	WHAT HE HEARS	TRY THIS, INSTEAD
That's not the right way.	*You're wrong.*	*What if you tried it this way?*

Can words really make that much of a difference? Once or twice, no. But over ten or fifteen years—yes! Your child will get impersonal, terse instructions from her friends, teachers and even strangers daily, so everything you can do to boost her self-confidence will help balance the negative messages he gets from other people.

Focus On the Positive.

I f your child has forgotten some of the reasons he's great, there are fun things you can do to help him remember. Start a habit of sharing something each morning that you like about yourself and ask him to share something he likes about himself, too.

If he can't think of something positive the first few times, ask him to tell you something he's happy about. Encourage him to talk about the good things that happened during the day. If you read the newspaper, notice the positive stories and make it a point to share them. Start a family journal and pass it around every night at dinner and ask everyone to add something good that happened to them that day. At the end of the week choose someone to read all the entries.

Listen to Your Child. Ask Questions to Encourage Her to Say More.

When you listen to your child you're giving her a gift that is priceless. Paying attention while she talks lets her know you think she's valuable and that what she says is interesting, worth knowing. Listening tells her you like her and are willing to spend time with her.

Whenever you can, stop what you're doing to listen. Look her in the eye. Avoid the temptation to interrupt or to finish her sentences. Let her finish before you share your own experience.

Really listen, even if you think you know what she's going to say, even though she may have told you once before. If you ask her questions and she frequently says, "I was just getting to that part," it may be a clue that you're rushing her through her story.

Teach Your Child to Be Honest.

A lthough we'd never expect children to learn to read overnight, we do seem to expect them to learn quickly how to be honest. But like reading, being honest is a learned skill, and some young children have an easier time understanding it than others.

Play a game together called Truth/Exaggeration/Lie. For example, you might say, "I have a black sweater [truth], it's the prettiest black sweater in the world [exaggeration] and I made it myself [lie]." Alternate the order of the statements so she has to think about which is the truth, which is the exaggeration and which is the lie.

Once a child understands what honesty is, the next step is to encourage her to choose to be honest. Tell her you appreciate her being honest when she is.

Do you know you can actually teach your child to be *dishonest?* You may not want to hear that she wishes her new sister or her grandma would go live with somebody else, and if you criticize her for saying so she will learn to say what she knows you want to hear instead of what's true.

If you get her to apologize for what she's said and she's still angry, her apology won't be honest. If she's punished for being honest about something she did wrong, she won't be very eager to tell the truth the next time.

She can learn a lot about honesty by seeing you be honest. If she sees an adult call in sick for work when he's not, or buy a child's admission when the child is overage, she'll get the idea that lying is okay if you don't get caught.

Practice What You Preach.

You probably grew up with parents who told you, "Do what I say, not what I do." You probably know that it doesn't work. You want your child to feel good about himself, so let him see that you feel good about yourself.

Let him see that you know you have talents and that you value them. Let him see that you accept compliments graciously. If something you try to do doesn't turn out the way you hoped, let him see that you understand it was the project that failed, not you.

If you tell of something embarrassing that happened at work, share a story about something you did that was successful, too.

Children learn a little by listening to our instructions and a lot by watching what we actually do.

Accept Her Offers of Help.

When your child offers to help, accept! Even if you know you could do the chore faster, even if you know you could do it better. When your child helps you she's showing that she wants to be with you and that she wants to please you—providing a golden opportunity to help boost her self-esteem when she succeeds.

Give her jobs that offer her an opportunity to show off her skills, and then don't be too fussy about the results.

Developing skills is a key to developing self-esteem and the more confident she feels, the more her self-esteem will rise. Even the youngest child can tear up the lettuce for a salad, set the table (none of the etiquette columnists will be there to check, so applaud her for her efforts) or sweep the porch.

Applaud His Efforts. Even the Messy Ones.

If someone were to ask us for the job definition of parent, we might say that it's to teach children what they need to learn in order to be successful. But while teaching is certainly a big part of parenting, it is only a part. Another part is allowing your child to develop on his own.

Think of how proud your child feels when he accomplishes something all by himself. Feeling proud of his accomplishments gives him confidence to try new things. That confidence to try new things is essential for children who live in a world that is constantly changing.

Applaud his efforts to make his own peanut butter sandwich, without making a big deal about the blobs that land on the counter. Applaud his efforts to help care for the pet, set the table or dust, even if he doesn't do the job as well as you could. The more successful he feels, the more successful he'll become.

Put Yourself in Your Child's Shoes.

I magine living in a world with people who are about twice your size, who know a lot more than you do and who make up all the rules. No matter how much you learn and how competent you become, they still tell you everything you can and cannot do.

This is what it's like for kids, and when you consider how well most of them put up with the situation, you have to hand it to them. They are more graceful than most adults would be.

Spend some time each day in your child's shoes. What, exactly, is she seeing? Is she seeing people who love and approve of her? Is she seeing people who make her feel safe and appreciated? Is she seeing people who approve of her just the way she is?

Karin Ireland

Look for ways to parent from your heart instead of your ego. Choose to be helpful instead of controlling. This does not mean that your child should do or have everything she wants (she shouldn't) or that there should not be rules (there should). However, there are ways to enforce rules that don't attack her, but rather help her learn.

Practice Having a Good Day.

When people wish you a good day you thank them for the thought and go on with what you were doing. But what if you actually *planned* to have a good day? Why not make it a family habit to practice having a good day?

At breakfast talk about the things each of you is looking forward to in the next few hours. Some days your child may have to think a while but you can help by asking questions that start her thinking: Is she looking forward to seeing a friend? Drawing or singing or playing a game at recess? It's good for her to learn she's in control, that she can *choose* to be happy.

Share the good parts of your day at dinner and plan your good day for tomorrow.

Karin Ireland

When Your Child Tells You
How He Feels,
Don't Tell Him How He *Should*
Feel Instead.

We mean to be helpful when we say things to our child like: Don't feel bad; don't feel rejected; don't feel hurt; don't feel sad or discouraged . . . don't feel what ever way you're feeling.

We want our child to feel better, but before he feels better, he needs to feel the feeling he's having.

Instead of rushing to push his feelings away, try to listen sympathetically. Add a wise "hmmm" from time to time. Maybe he just needs to be heard before he can move on.

If he seems stuck in a feeling and he's made it clear that he wants to move on, help him explore ways he might be able to let go. He might choose something pleasant that he can think about when the other unwanted feeling comes up. Journaling might help him let these feelings slip away.

Or he can focus on the feeling, notice where it is in his body and then imagine what shape it is. After he knows the shape, he can move it out of his body, turn it into mist and watch it float away. You can also help him craft affirmations that remind him that all is well.

Encourage Your Child to Talk About What She Wants Instead of What She Doesn't.

We used to tell children not to complain because it didn't do any good, and besides, other people got tired of hearing it. That's true, but there's another reason they shouldn't complain: People tend to get what they think about most. What your child thinks about will affect what happens in her life. Someone once said, "Whether you think you can or you can't, you're right."

A person who has high self-esteem has a good sense of being able to control many of the important parts of her life, and when your child talks about what she wants and then looks for ways to succeed, she'll feel like she's in control. By talking about the positive things in her life she'll begin to notice how many there are!

Let It Be Okay for Your Child to Disagree.

When our children are young they hang on our every word. We are the undeniable experts. And being adored is addictive.

There'll come a time, though, when your child will begin to disagree with you, and it's valuable for her to learn to be able to sometimes disagree with people who are important to her. It's a skill that will help her say no to peers who want her to do things that are unsafe or unkind.

Let her know that it's okay for her to like a movie you don't, to enjoy things you don't, even to like people you don't care for. There will be times when you remember an event one way and she remembers it another. No amount of discussion will convince the other, and the best solution is just to agree to disagree.

Karin Ireland

Show Your Child You're a "Can Do" Family.

E very family has challenges, and sometimes they can seem nearly overwhelming. But it is important for a child's growing self-esteem that he feels his family can pull together, that his has optimism and plans to overcome whatever difficulties they find themselves facing.

Don't share details with a very young child if they could be frightening, but do let him know in general terms what's going on. If he's old enough, invite him to sit in on discussions between you and your spouse or let him help work toward a solution.

Single parents are families, too. If you're a single parent, be positive about your future. Let him see how you make decisions, how you make plans for success.

Know the Values You Want
Your Child to Have.

What are some of the key values you want to teach your child? Honesty? Independence? Self-reliance? Tolerance? An open mind? Once you have a list, look for ways to teach these values.

If you want her to be independent, encourage her to make her own decisions (even if some are different from what you think they should be), encourage her to think for herself (even if she thinks the opposite of you) and encourage her to honor her beliefs even if her friends all disagree with them.

If you want her to be self-reliant, avoid rushing in to help her get out of a jam. One of the ways to teach her to be tolerant and open-minded is by being tolerant and having an open mind yourself. When you see or hear about situations where people have been intolerant, ask her what she thinks she might have done in the same situation.

What are other values you want to teach? Here are a few: integrity, compassion, reliability, fairness, generosity, helpfulness, perseverance, responsibility, commitment, courage and thankfulness.

Demonstrate the Values You Want Your Child to Have.

"Values are caught, not taught," said the late Lawrence Kohlberg, a Harvard psychologist who studied moral development in children. Your child "catches" values by watching you.

He learns about honesty by seeing you tell the clerk that she gave you too much change and by hearing you tell a neighbor that you'd rather not do what she wants you to instead of making up an excuse.

He learns about forgiveness by seeing you forgive someone who has hurt you, and he learns about compassion by seeing ways that you are willing to help others without judging.

Karin Ireland

Pick a Value Each Week and Practice It Every Day.

Think of a value you believe someone with high self-esteem has and encourage the whole family to practice it every day. At the end of the week choose a new value. Here are some values you might use: honesty, courage, loyalty, patience, respect, responsibility, cooperation, humor, tolerance, self-reliance, independence, empathy and kindness.

People have noticed that when you vow to demonstrate a value—for example, to be patient—dozens of things will happen in the next few days to challenge your patience. Try to appreciate the opportunity to practice and then have a family laugh about the "coincidence."

Don't Make Your Child Feel Guilty for Wanting What She Wants or for Being Who She Is.

K ids go through a time when it seems they want everything and believe they should have it. They shouldn't, of course, and sometimes it gets frustrating when they keep asking. When we get frustrated, we're likely to get angry at them for putting us in the position of always having to say no.

But our anger can send them messages that there are things they should want and things they shouldn't. Instead of being free to want what they want, they may begin to feel guilty. They'll wonder, "Am I being unreasonable if I ask for this? Will I seem greedy or unappreciative by asking for more than I already have? What will people think of me if I ask?" Life then becomes a guessing game as they try to feel what is appropriate instead of what is real.

Say Yes Whenever You Can.

S ay yes to your child whenever you can. That doesn't mean not to say no when you need to—it means not to say no when you're rushed or hungry or in a bad mood. At those times, let him know it's not a good time to ask and invite him to ask again later.

What does saying yes have to do with self-esteem? It sends the message, You're important. You're valuable. You have a right to want what you want. (Note that that does not mean that he's always going to get it! See the next tip.)

Help Him Learn to Be Okay with "No."

While it's true that your child should be able to ask for what he wants, he also needs to be okay with not getting everything.

One way you can help make it easier when you do say no is to say it kindly, the way you'd want him to say no to you.

Let Your Child Know She's Special to You.

Remember how special you thought she was when she took her first step or said her first word? It was your delighted encouragement that kept her walking even though she fell a lot; it was your encouragement that kept her practicing new sounds until she managed to learn an entire language.

Chances are you still think she's special, but chances are you forget to let her know. Chances are you could still inspire her to learn things she doesn't think she can learn, to push past temporary setbacks to ultimate success.

Leave her notes in her room, in her lunch, in the mail that applaud her for something she did or something she is that you think is great. Start a tradition of telling her every night at bedtime one way she's special to you.

Give Gifts That Boost
Self-Esteem.

1. Make a book and write down 101 things you love about your child and then give it to her as a birthday or holiday gift. Of course, you don't have to stop at 101 . . .

2. Make a video or audiotape of friends telling why he's their friend.

3. Make an audiotape of you saying why you're glad she's your daughter.

4. Send a card that says "I'm glad you're part of my life," "I love knowing you" or some other positive message.

5. Look for gifts that relate to an interest of his, a gift that adds to a collection or in some other way shows you enjoy making him happy.

Teach Your Child to Appreciate the Difference Between People.

People who are different can enrich your child's life by exposing him to new traditions and ideas. Exploring the beliefs and behaviors of people who are different can open doors to new thinking that can lead to possibilities he might not have thought of otherwise.

Being with people who are different can be fun, too. And when he realizes that it's okay for other people to be different, he'll realize it's okay for him to be different in some ways, too.

Encourage Your Child to Ask Questions About Rules and Ethical Decisions.

D on't wait for the next political scandal to talk—to your child about rules and ethics—look for opportunities every day.

If your child asks why you have certain rules in your family, be willing to explain. Why shouldn't she just follow the rules because you told her to? It's true, she should do what you tell her to do, but it's also true that your goal is to teach her how to make the right decisions on her own, too. The more she understands the reasons for rules, the more she'll be able to make good decisions by herself.

Tell her about some of the rules at your workplace and encourage her to ask questions about them. Talk to her about the ethics our society considers important (like honesty, fair play and kindness) and encourage her to ask questions.

Help Your Child Realize He Has Choices.

Success requires enthusiasm, because being successful takes work! Children—and adults—are more able to do that work when they feel they are in control of at least some areas of their life.

Give your child choices about when to do chores and even, whenever possible, which ones to do. Let him decide what to wear and which extracurricular activities to participate in.

Ask "choice" questions like, "Would you rather feed the dog now or after dinner? Should we rent a movie or go to the library? Would you like to have hamburgers or pizza?"

Feeling he has some control over his life will contribute to his self-esteem and will also train him to make more important decisions as he gets older.

Start with the End in Mind.

R aising a child is a project, and with any successful project, it's important to start with the end in mind. What kind of person do you want your child to be? Happy? Confident? Independent? Responsible? Loyal? Kind? Honest? Willing to take risks?

Make a list and once you know what you want her to be, write down all the things you can do to help her.

Then make a list of the things you're already doing that will help.

Next, write down the things you're doing that might make it difficult for your child to develop a desired trait.

Write down things you aren't doing that you could be doing.

Karin Ireland

And, finally, put a check in front of the things you'll start or stop doing today.

Try to think about the end you want for your child every month or so, because she and the situations she finds herself in will change often as she grows up.

Encourage Your Child to Be Creative About Getting What He Wants.

S ometimes, when our child asks for more than we're willing or able to give him, we get frustrated and criticize him for asking and tell him to be happy with what he has. But if everyone was happy with what he had we'd still be lighting fires by rubbing two sticks together.

In order to succeed in today's world, a child needs to know how to be persistent, to know how to go after what he wants and to keep working until he gets it.

That doesn't mean he should keep asking you until you give in, but rather that he should think of other ways he might be able to get what he wants.

If what he wants takes money, can he do extra chores for you and be paid? Can he do chores for one of the neighbors?

Karin Ireland

If what he wants takes time—*your* time—and you don't have it, can he do some of your chores so you will have time?

Someone once said that more than talent or luck, persistence leads to success. Creative persistence is how great people get what they want.

Don't Use Shame to Control Your Child.

S hame is defined as a state of disgrace or dishonor and is a pretty powerful and negative emotion. Some parents use shame to control their child simply because it is so powerful that it subdues him. But a child's feeling disgraced and dishonored is not good for her self-esteem.

Instead of using shame, look for other ways to teach your child the lessons you believe she needs to learn. Set good examples. Talk about people who set good examples. Realize that your child is a work in progress and that some days she (like the adults in her life) will forget some of the lessons that she's learned.

Karin Ireland

Show Respect for Your Spouse or Partner.

Your child will learn a great deal by watching the way the adults in his life behave. It's easier for a child to feel self-respect when the adults in his life respect each other.

If you and your spouse have slipped into a pattern of disrespect, talk about it and see if you can agree to be more respectful. If you need marriage counseling, get it. Your child will unconsciously mimic the relationship habits he sees now when he grows up, so you can give him a great gift by showing how well relationships can work.

Teach Basic Good Manners and Demonstrate Them.

T he more your child understands what's expected of him, the more comfortable he'll be, and that boosts his self-esteem. Right or wrong, some people will judge him by the way they see him behave, and that's not fair to him if he doesn't even know what good manners are.

Teach him the basics of saying "Please" and "Thank you," not interrupting while others are talking, not bolting through an open door before everyone else, not blowing his nose at meals, not slurping food or beverages and not talking with his mouth full.

Encourage Your Child's Sense of Humor.

P eople like to be around people who laugh, and so when you encourage your child's sense of humor, you help her develop a relationship skill that will boost her self-esteem.

Encourage her sense of humor by appreciating her jokes and clever comments. Go to the library together and choose some joke books and try to discover the secrets of what makes a joke funny. Watch comedies on TV, go to funny movies and look for books that are humorous. Be a good role model—let her see your sense of humor, too.

If it seems as if your child is uncomfortable calling attention to herself, it may be because she doesn't know what's expected of her and so she doesn't know what to do. Practice telling jokes from the library books to each other. After a while she may be more comfortable speaking up in other situations, and in the meantime she's having fun and beginning to recognize the value of humor.

Make Most of Your Interactions with Your Child Positive.

Everyone's overly busy these days, and when you're tired it's easy to slip into a mode of just trying to get everything done in time to get in bed so you can get up and do it again. Sometimes a parent may move through the evening like a project manager and only stop to talk to his child when giving instructions or criticisms.

If you notice this happening, make a list of all the projects you're trying to get done at home and then eliminate several of them so you have time to enjoy your child. When he's grown up and ready to leave home you'll be more likely to think about all the lost opportunities you had to be with him than about all the projects you got done while he waited patiently for you to finish.

Ask yourself sometimes what the greatest mistake you could make with your child would be. It wouldn't be that you didn't teach him how to make his bed every morning. It would be that you lost the heart-to-heart connection.

Karin Ireland

Don't Tell Your Child His Fears Are Silly.

S o many of the things we tell our children are meant to be helpful but aren't, really.

When we tell a child that his fears are silly we mean to reassure him; we're saying that he really doesn't have anything to worry about. But what the child hears is that you're not taking his feelings seriously. Or, he may learn that he can't trust his feelings to be true.

Instead of telling him his fears are silly, encourage him to talk about them and then ask him questions that help him understand why he has them. If he realizes that something he's been afraid of has never happened, he may decide that it probably never will.

Help him discover what he can do to minimize the likelihood of his fears coming true. In case they did, ask him, what would he do? And what could he do to make sure those things never happened again?

Smile at Your Child, and Hug Her.

S miles are the universal language of friendship and love and they're a simple way to send your child a message of approval.

Noted psychologist Virginia Satir says a person needs four hugs a day for survival, eight for maintenance and sixteen for growth!

Take time every day to smile and hug your child—it's as good for you as it is for her!

Karin Ireland

Assume She's Right Before You Assume She's Wrong.

When a child is very young we assume we know more than she does, and it's true, we do. But at some point the child learns things we don't know and has perceptions about events that are different from ours, and if we forget this, we may assume she's wrong whenever her answers don't seem logical or when they aren't consistent with what's happened in the past.

You can help her feel competent by being willing to give her the benefit of the doubt and by asking her questions to clarify what she means instead of telling her she's wrong.

Show Your Child How to Ask for Help.

We used to think that asking for help was a sign of weakness, but now we know that it's a sign of strength. We recognize that someone who can ask for help has enough confidence to be able to admit he doesn't have all the answers and that he is anxious to learn.

Ask your child for his help from time to time. Accept help when he offers, even if you could do the chore alone.

Applaud Improvement.

L ook for opportunities to celebrate improvements and resist the urge to point out that there is still room for more.

Eliminate Words That Hurt.

Some family members may use hurtful words to express anger and some may use them thinking they will motivate a child to change a behavior. Hurtful words damage self-esteem because even though the child may argue that they aren't true . . . she wonders if maybe they are.

Encourage your family and friends to eliminate phrases like: Big boys don't cry; don't be a sissy; girls can't do that; girls shouldn't do that; you're lazy, stupid or a mama's boy; you're fat, sloppy or uncoordinated; I don't know what I'm going to do with you; you're hopeless, helpless, ungrateful or never going to amount to anything.

Karin Ireland

Encourage Your Child's Questions.

A child who feels competent has good self-esteem, and one way a child develops a sense of competency is by asking questions. Answer his questions the best way you can and if you're stumped, suggest you both go to the library and look for a book or see what you can find on the Internet.

It's true, a constant stream of questions can be annoying sometimes, so when they are, why not ask for a break instead of ignoring your child. Being ignored will make him feel that he isn't very important and if you get impatient, he may decide that questions aren't okay.

But if you explain that this really isn't a good time for a lot of questions and you'd like to answer them when you get home or after dinner, you'll be teaching him to be flexible and patient and you'll be letting him know that the timing is bad, but the questions are fine.

Don't Assume Your Child Knows What to Do.

When you ask your child to dust the table or mop the floor or rake the leaves, *you* know you mean for him to move the magazines instead of just dusting around them, to mop under the table as well as the open spaces and to rake the leaves into a pile and then put them into the trash.

But your child may not know unless you've told him at an earlier time. Or he may know and figure that since you didn't tell him to do that you might not mind if he doesn't.

If your child regularly misses a step or two of a chore, remind him what you need him to do, with words that don't make him feel lazy or stupid.

Karin Ireland

Examine Gender Stereotypes with Your Child.

In a perfect world, boys and girls, men and women would not put unkind labels on each other because of their gender. In the real world, it's hard to go a day without hearing one or the other sex get slammed: "You run like a girl" or "Boys don't cry," sports coaches calling boys "girls" to shame them after a bad performance, men telling "blonde" jokes (of course they don't mean blonde men) and so on.

Gender stereotypes hurt both sexes, and your child may be hearing these labeling comments at school and accepting them as true. It is unlikely he will not be affected by these gender labels, because almost everybody fits into one of the categories under attack.

Talk about gender stereotypes with your child and ask if he believes they're true. If he does, why does he? Encourage him to tell you when he hears them so you can counteract those messages with positive ones.

Be Willing to Explain
Bad Words.

I t's inevitable—someday your child is going to ask you what a dirty word means. You may be surprised that he's heard the word or you may be embarrassed at the thought of having to explain it, but please don't be angry with him for asking. It's better for him to get information from you than from someone who might explain it in a way you wouldn't approve of.

Teach Your Child to Visualize What She Wants Instead of What She Doesn't.

There are whole books about visualization, and we think of it as a new technique, but the truth is that your child has been doing it most of her life.

Unfortunately, most of the time she visualizes what she doesn't want instead of what she does. She visualizes the teacher being mad at her if she doesn't get a good grade on her report, she visualizes her classmates laughing if she makes a mistake when she answers a question and she visualizes a friend turning down an invitation.

Help her learn to visualize positive scenes instead. If she's due to give a report and worries that she'll seem foolish, encourage her to picture herself being a tremendous success, even getting a standing ovation at the end. Of course, she also has to do the work, but having a positive attitude will make that seem easier, too.

Change your own visualizations to positive ones and talk about them. Let her hear you looking forward to being successful on your next driving test or your next assignment at work instead of worrying.

Will It Matter Ten Years from Now?

Y ou've probably noticed the cycle: Your child is doing all the things that annoy you and you're annoying her by pointing them all out. The more annoyed you get, the more she does things that annoy you. Somebody has to stop the cycle, and it usually has to be the grown-up.

You might start by letting her know that you're frustrated with your relationship right now, but that you're going to look for ways to get it back on track and if she thinks of anything she can do to help, that would be great.

Then look for things you can do. Start noticing opportunities to compliment her on something she's doing well. Ask yourself, "Will it matter ten years from now (if she knows how to make a perfect bed, if she uses the same system you do to wash the dishes, that she missed a spot when she wiped the kitchen counter)?" And if it won't, let it go.

Enjoy Your Child.

Hug him, kiss him, laugh at his jokes, really look at his drawings, listen to his songs, ask him to tell you a story, go with him to the movies, play games that nobody wins. Take him to the zoo, go on a picnic, swim at the beach, build sand castles, learn to do yo-yo tricks together, split a hot-fudge sundae. Laugh with him, sing with him, dance with him, let him know you think he's fun to be with.

Communicate Clearly.

I f you and your child often disagree about what one of you said, what one of you meant, what one of you promised to do, chances are you could both be communicating more clearly.

If she often forgets to do something you've asked her to, it may be that she doesn't remember things she hears as well as she remembers things she sees. Try writing her a note.

If, on the other hand, you leave her notes to do things and she doesn't see them, she might be a person who doesn't rely heavily on her visual sense and might do better if she hears the message.

When you ask her to do something, ask her to repeat what you said or to write herself a note.

Let Go of Old Mistakes.

N o one likes to hear about their mistakes, and they like it even less when they have to hear about ones that should have been buried long ago. Try to make sure that when you reach back into the past you reach for a time when your child succeeded rather than a time when he didn't.

Let Your Child Help Make Family Decisions.

S tudies show that employees who have some control over their work are happier and more productive than those who don't, and the same thing is true with children. A child who feels that she matters, that she has something to say about how the family is run, feels empowered.

While it wouldn't be appropriate for her to decide things like whether to buy a new car or not, she can help decide family matters like where to go for a vacation, what to do over the weekend and what to name the new pet.

Encourage Your Child to Keep a Success Journal.

Unless you plan to raise your child on a deserted island, she's likely to be around people who will make her feel like she's not as successful as others are. If she hears it too often she may start to believe it's true and once she does, she'll consciously or unconsciously expect to fail.

She can counteract other people's negative messages by remembering ways she's successful. Encourage her to keep a success journal, something she writes in every night.

At first she might need you to help her identify successes. Was she able to sit still when the teacher asked her to? That's a success. Did she remember to feed the dog without being asked? That's a success. Did she listen to a friend who needed to talk to her? That's a success. Pretty soon it'll be easy for her to recognize ways that she is successful and to add them to her journal by herself.

Help Your Child Fit In.

While it's true that self-esteem comes from inside, it's also true that positive feedback from teachers and peers can help.

If your child is overweight, encourage him to exercise, eat raw vegetables for snacks, go easy on the starches and eliminate most of the sugar in his diet. If he's uncomfortable speaking up in class, hold practice sessions at home. Help him gather facts about something the other kids talk about, like sports, music or the hottest (nonviolent) video games.

If he lags behind his classmates in reading or math, talk to his teacher and get a tutor if necessary.

Treat Your Child the Way You'd Treat a Special Friend.

B ecause our kids live with us day after day, we may sometimes forget to use our "company manners" when we talk to them and when we respond to their needs.

Talk to your child kindly, and if you're not in the mood to do that tell her so and ask her to leave you alone while you get in a better mood. Look for ways to say yes more often than you say no. Honor your child's trust. Respect your child and her privacy. Say "Please" and "Thank you" and smile.

Teach Your Child to Set Goals.

Everyone who is successful had a goal first. Jumping into a project without having a goal is like starting a trip without having a destination. You'll end up someplace, but where? And how will you know when you get there?

Help your child explore areas where goals might be beneficial. Is there a subject she'd like to improve on in school? What level of competency does she want to achieve? What does she need to do to reach it? How will she know when she does? What is a small reward she can give herself every few months for staying focused?

She can have goals to improve in sports and she might make it a goal to remember to do her chores. She might have a goal to learn to play the guitar or to get a summer job.

Some goals can be short-term—things she wants to accomplish in a week. Others might be goals she'll work on for a month or a year. She may even have goals for when she grows up.

Consciously thinking about goals, planning how to achieve them and then following through will make her feel like she's in control of her life. And that's a great feeling for her to have.

Affirmations Help Boost
Self-Esteem.

ffirmations—positive messages we tell ourselves—
are something we hear a lot about these days, but
they're not new. Kids use them every day, but unfortunately they
usually affirm what they don't want instead of what they do. "I
can't do that; I'm no good at sports; I'm no good at math; I'll
probably flunk that test; I'm not smart enough, big enough, old
enough, tall enough. . . ." And pretty soon, they start to believe
that what they tell themselves is true.

How do you help your child change the habit? One way is
by talking about it, helping her understand the habit she's gotten
into and thinking of ways she can change. For example, instead
of saying to herself, "I'm no good at math," she can start saying
something that is positive (and true), like, "Sometimes I really

understand math. I bet I will understand it better as I learn more."

Encourage her to notice when her teachers and friends fall into this negative habit and then to make a conscious decision not to participate in it. She doesn't need to contradict them; instead she can say something to herself like, "But that isn't true for me."

Make a daily affirmation a family ritual. Post a new one on the refrigerator door each morning and encourage everyone to use the affirmation several times that day.

A note about affirmations: Keep them positive and in the present—as if they've already been accomplished. "Today I easily attract all the information I need. Today my mind is clear and I remember everything I need to. Today I do a great job on all my projects."

Can this really work? Oprah Winfrey proved how strong the power of suggestion is with one of her studio audiences. When people arrived, they were told that there would be an odor released in the lobby and they'd be asked to identify it. The message was repeated several times and finally they were told the odor had been released.

Staff asked dozens of people what it smelled like to them and nearly everyone had an opinion. Some even complained of a choking feeling, nausea or slight difficulty in breathing.

Once seated, the audience was told that an odor hadn't really been released—it was an experiment to test how suggestible people were.

Five Positive Affirmations Your Child Can Use to Boost Her Self-Esteem.

1. Math (spelling, history, etc.) just seems to get easier for me every week.

2. I always seem to be able to figure out what I need to know in order to do what I need to do.

3. Every day I notice several big or little ways I am successful.

4. Sometimes I amaze myself with all the things I know.

5. I get better every day at remembering the things I need to remember.

Attack the Problem,
Not the Child.

Haim Ginott offered this message in the early seventies in his book *Between Parent and Child*, and it's still a good message nearly thirty years later.

Look for ways to let your child know the action or behavior you want instead of attacking him for not meeting your expectations. For example, "There are still a lot of things on your bedroom floor and I think you can find someplace to put them where they'll be out of sight" gives your child a clear message of what you expect without attacking him and is much better for his self-esteem than "Can't you see this room is still a mess?" which is an attack on him.

When you say what you want to have happen, and sound like you know he can do it, your good attitude and positive language can motivate him to do a better job.

Team Sports Can Boost Self-Esteem.

Playing a sport that he can eventually become competent in will help your child develop physical strength and courage, will help him learn to be assertive and will help him develop leadership skills. It's said that men have an advantage in the work world because of the relationship skills they learned on sports teams, and now girls have the same opportunities.

Notice how he's getting along in the sport, because playing one that is wrong for his body type or skills could have a negative effect on him physically and, if he's seriously mismatched, could damage his self-esteem.

Teach Your Child That Neatness Counts.

I t may not be fair, but it's often true that a neat paper receives a higher grade than a sloppy paper that might contain better information. One reason is that the neat paper is easier to read! If a teacher can't read a child's handwriting, the material won't seem as worthy and the writing won't flow.

Instead of telling children to write a paper, teachers should probably tell them to write a paper and then recopy it in their neatest handwriting. But even if the teachers don't, you can and should if your child is satisfied with a sloppy paper. Until you're certain your child understands how to do writing assignments neatly, ask to see them.

Math is another subject where neatness counts. Every day children have correct answers marked as incorrect because the teacher couldn't read them!

Karin Ireland

Help Your Child Value Who He Is More Than What He Does.

A ccomplishments are terrific and your child should be proud of all the skills he has, but even more important than what he does is who he is. If he is kind, patient, tolerant, persistent, trusting, enthusiastic, optimistic and in other ways someone who has positive behaviors, he should be very proud of himself.

Don't Compare Your Child with Other People.

In order to develop good self-esteem, children need to feel good about who they are, and comparing them with someone else, especially if you're hinting that the other person is more successful, won't nurture that feeling.

Instead, praise your child for who she is and if you offer suggestions for improvement base them on her own unique potential.

Catch Your Child in the Act of Doing Something Right and Make It a Big Deal.

There's a joke about a child who doesn't talk until he's quite old and whose first words are a complete sentence—a complaint about breakfast. His astonished parents ask why he's never spoken before, and he answers that up until this moment everything has been fine.

It's easy for parents to fall into the habit of expecting everything to be fine and only pointing out the times when it isn't, but your child needs to have more positive than negative feedback.

Let him know you appreciate his efforts and that you admire his success. If it's a really big success, call a relative and brag about him. Make sure you call when he will overhear you boasting.

Encourage Your Child to Share Her Successes with You.

In order for your child to have high self-esteem, it's important for her to recognize all the ways she's successful. Let her know that it's perfectly okay to brag to you.

"Sandwich" Complaints Can Backfire.

The person who thought up sandwiching complaints had a good idea, but sometimes even the best ideas backfire. A sandwich complaint is one you tuck in the middle of two honest compliments. For example: I really like the writing style of your book report (compliment) but I think you could have included more details about the main character's reason for selling her horse (complaint). Still, your handwriting was very neat and it was easy for me to read your report (compliment).

The good thing about this style is that you offer your child some positive messages even though you have a negative one tucked in there, too. The disadvantage is that if you use it regularly she will begin to expect that every compliment is going to be followed with a complaint. Instead of being able to bask in the praise, she'll be wondering what complaint you're about to make.

Why not try leaving off the first compliment so that what she hears is the complaint and then the compliment.

Don't Confuse a Quiet Child with a Good Child.

There's no doubt about it, a quiet child can be less trouble and easier to be around—and so we think that a quiet child is a good child. But a quiet child can also be a child who doesn't feel comfortable competing for a place in the conversation. A quiet child can be uncertain about what she wants to say or might be afraid that her words will be misunderstood.

There are times when being quiet is appropriate (during rest periods, when someone else is talking, events) and other times when she needs to be asking questions and sharing her ideas in order to learn and develop self-confidence.

If your child tends to be quiet, look for ways to draw her out. Set aside special times to talk to her and to let her tell you about her day, her friends, the work she did in school.

Rethink Some of Your Beliefs About Parenting.

E very once in a while, stop and think about your be-liefs on parenting. Are they mostly positive? Do they seem to be working? Does your child appear to be thriving?

Think of parenting as an ongoing project that needs to be fine-tuned from time to time. Reread this book—you'll notice different tips each time you do, depending on what's happening in your family.

Talk to like-minded parents about what works or doesn't work for them. Ignore people who warn you about the difficult ages and phases your child will go through—some children do and many don't.

Be willing to let go of rules, routines and beliefs that don't seem to be working; be open to learning new ways to teach, support and foster self-esteem.

Encourage Your Child to Try Things Just for Fun.

A child who becomes too determined to be a success might not be willing to try something new unless he believes he can master it. Help your child understand that there are many things that he should do just for fun. Much of life is about balance, and you can help him learn how to decide which things need to be mastered and which don't.

One child may decide that he has a passion for soccer and will do whatever he can to master the sport. Another child may just enjoy the game as an activity and feel no need to excel. In that case, he should do his best during the game and in practice and then be happy with whatever the result is.

Play games with him, and don't always keep score. Let him see you try new activities without getting frustrated if you don't succeed.

A child who believes he needs to master everything he attempts will be frustrated, because for most people, it just isn't possible.

Respect Your Child. Be Someone She Can Respect.

B eing comfortable in a family is a good thing—until someone becomes so comfortable that he or she forgets to talk and act with respect toward other family members.

It's never too early to show your child respect. At the earliest ages, you show respect when you talk lovingly to your child, when you listen to her needs and do what you can to take care of them.

As she gets older, you show your respect by listening without interrupting when she talks, by recognizing that she might have a valid complaint sometimes, by treating her the way you'd like to be treated or the way you treat your best friend.

You show your respect by honoring her wishes whenever you can, by honoring her space (her room), by not intruding without knocking and by taking her worries and complaints seriously.

The fun part is that when you act respectfully toward her, she can see you as someone to respect.

Karin Ireland

Be a Good Role Model of the Attitudes You Want Your Child to Have.

S omeone once said that despite our best efforts to teach children good manners, they mimic their parents anyway. It's not just our manners they pick up, but our attitudes as well.

Consider the attitudes that you think are the most important ones to have and then look for ways you can demonstrate them in front of your child. Look for ways he can see you being optimistic, open-minded, forgiving, patient, understanding and flexible. Look for times when his attitude is great and compliment him.

Encourage Your Child to Be a Good Listener.

L istening is more than just being polite—it can help a person gather information, solve problems and even stay out of trouble! When you encourage the habit of good listening you give your child a valuable gift.

Someone who won't listen runs the risk of alienating other people and misses information that could help her or even save her from a serious mistake.

There are several ways you can encourage your child to listen: Read her stories she wants to hear, talk to her about things she's interested in, keep most of your messages positive. Notice if her attention starts to lag and if it does, change the subject, change the activity or just take a break.

Help Your Child Be Positive About the Future.

A child who believes that there are good things to look forward to in the future will be happy and more willing to work hard to learn what she needs to learn now.

Encourage her to plan things to look forward to. Encourage her daydreams about what she wants to be when she grows up. Of course, she'll probably change her mind a dozen times before she's actually ready for a career, but in the meantime she'll have fun exploring possibilities. Encourage her to have fun things to look forward to next week, next month and next year, too.

Expect Your Child to Succeed.

S uccess coaches teach that we get what we put our attention on, and if this is true we'll be better off if we put our attention on things we want rather than on things we don't want.

When you expect your child to succeed, you boost her self-esteem and confidence. When you expect her to succeed she'll begin to believe she can, too. Even at those times when she doesn't seem to have reached the goal she was aiming for, help her realize that she succeeded in *trying* and is closer to reaching that goal next time.

Nurture Your Child's Special Gifts.

D oes your child like to draw or write or sing or dance? Is he funny or clever or does he have an interest in drama, science or nature? Does he have a great memory? Is he a natural comedian?

Talk to him about the things he likes to do and the things he does well. Surprise him with books from the library on the subjects he's interested in; read them yourself so you can share his enthusiasm.

If he's good at math, ask him to help you choose the best buy when you go shopping. Ask him to double-check your figures when you balance the checking account. If he likes to draw, invite him to design your greeting cards or create wrapping paper. If he's a good listener, a good friend, maybe he'd enjoy joining a mentor group at school.

Provide a Home That Is
Physically Safe.

S ad to say, but not all grown-ups can be trusted. You can't even trust some family members. Help your child—boy or girl—understand which kind of touching is appropriate and which isn't. Let her know you want her to tell you if someone says or does something that makes her uncomfortable. Talk to her if her behavior changes, if she becomes nervous or moody or withdrawn.

The world is a scary place for kids these days. Check, double-check and triple-check the qualifications and references of anyone you hire to take care of your child. Spend time every evening talking to her about what happened during the day. Ask leading questions about what people said and how they acted. If it sounds like something inappropriate has happened, investigate; don't assume she's exaggerating.

Talk to your child about what you want her to do if someone she knows behaves inappropriately, if someone she doesn't know approaches her when she's alone, if someone comes to school with a weapon.

Talk to her about what you want her to do if there's a sudden storm, earthquake or other natural disaster while she's en route to school or alone at home.

Bring the subject up again from time to time and invite her to ask questions.

Provide a Home That Is Emotionally Safe.

S ome jokes are real knee-slappers . . . except to the person who is the butt of the humor. Some sibling rivalry is probably inescapable, but if its zings are meant to wound, they probably will.

Try to learn why the attacker needs to attack and look for ways to rectify that.

Say Thank You.

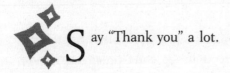S ay "Thank you" a lot.

Teach Your Child to Think Before She Makes a Promise.

It's easy for her to make a promise without thinking and then later realize that she can't honor it. Sometimes she may make a promise because she feels obligated by the person asking or she wants to seem nice or helpful or agreeable. She may break that promise later or may honor it resentfully.

Help her learn to think about a promise before she makes it. She can notice how her body feels and get valuable clues about whether she wants to do a particular favor. She should think about her schedule and see if she has the time to do it. If she can't decide, she can ask for time; if the person asking says there isn't any, it may be better for her to decline.

There's a good opportunity to be a role model here by not

Karin Ireland

letting anyone, even your daughter, push you to make promises you aren't comfortable making. When she sees you stop to think, to ask for time if needed and to decline those requests you don't feel comfortable with, she'll begin to see how she can do the same thing.

Be a Detective.

Behavior has a message and if your child is behaving in a way that's inappropriate, discover what the message is.

If he's unusually angry, why is he? Does he feel left out, is he feeling overwhelmed? If he's misbehaving at school, could it be because he's having trouble with his lessons and trying to cover it up? Is he having trouble seeing the chalkboard or hearing the teacher?

If he's quiet or moody, is he feeling alone? Is something bothering him that he doesn't know how to handle?

Simply saying, "What's the matter with you?" is likely to bring the response, "Nothing." Instead, stop doing other chores and focus on him. Say things like, "It seems to me you're feeling

Karin Ireland

more (fill in the behavior) these days and I know that when that happens to me it sometimes helps to talk about it. Sometimes when I talk to people who care, they help me find a solution."

If he doesn't volunteer information, ask a question that assumes he eventually will and that lets him know you'll be there to listen. For example, "Would you like to talk to me about it now or would you rather wait a while?"

Eat Dinner Together
Every Night.

One study has revealed that 50 percent of Americans keep the TV on during family dinners. And another, by the U.S. Department of Education, has shown that children who talk about current events at home tend to be higher achievers at school.

Dinnertime is a great opportunity to talk to each other, to share what happened during the day. It gives everyone a chance to reconnect, and it's a good time to compliment your child on something he did, said or is.

Don't Redo the Things Your Child Does.

I t's so tempting to "touch up" your child's work—to redust the spot she missed on the table, to rewipe the kitchen counter, to readjust the way she positioned the books, the pillows, the flowers—but don't. It sends a clear and demotivating message that she didn't do the job "right." Instead, ask yourself these questions: Is there a health or safety issue here? Will this matter in ten years? If you answer no, then ask yourself another question: Just this one time, can I let go of my need for things to be perfect?

Give Your Child Chores to Do
That Boost His Self-Esteem.

It's tempting to ask your child to do the tasks that you don't like to do or ones that you know he can accomplish without making a mess. But chores have a great potential to boost your child's self-esteem. Let him choose some of his own chores so he'll be motivated to do them. Let him do ones that help him learn new skills or that make him feel more like one of the big kids.

Appreciate his efforts and applaud him for doing a good job even if it isn't done as perfectly as you'd have liked it to be. He'll feel good because of your enthusiasm and he may want to improve and do it even better!

Karin Ireland

Ten Ways You Can Raise Your Child's Self-Esteem.

1. Praise him.

2. Respect her opinions, even if you disagree.

3. Ask for his advice.

4. Notice when she does something well and comment on it.

5. Tell him you love him.

6. Let her be appropriately independent.

7. Monitor his schoolwork and get him help if he needs it.

8. Be positive, and encourage her to be positive, too.

9. Expect him to succeed.

10. Guide her to activities in which she will succeed.

Ten Things That Can Lower Your Child's Self-Esteem.

1. Parents' or other family members' disapproval.

2. Parents fighting; divorce; an uncertain future.

3. Difficulties with friends.

4. A change in friends.

5. Difficulties with a teacher.

6. Difficulties with schoolwork.

7. Negative family members or friends.

8. A move to a new home, neighborhood or school.

9. Believing that he is different in a negative way.

10. Criticism.

Karin Ireland

Look for Discipline That Teaches Instead of Punishes.

For some reason many people think that discipline and punishment mean the same thing. But in the dictionary the original definition of discipline is "training."

A couple of generations ago parents believed they needed to control their children, to teach them by whatever means it took to adhere to a rigid set of behaviors. But rigid obedience doesn't prepare a child to be successful in today's world, and so teaching a child how to make good decisions on her own is more important than teaching her to follow a nonnegotiable set of rules.

The discipline that is most effective (and promotes the highest self-esteem) is one that is the natural outcome of the unwanted behavior.

For example, if a child breaks a lamp as a result of doing

something she wasn't supposed to be doing, the punitive response might be to take away a privilege or to ground her for a week. The natural-outcome approach would be to make her be responsible for at least part of the replacement of the lamp by either contributing a part of her allowance to the purchase of a new one or by doing extra chores in exchange for the money you will have to pay to replace it.

If a child hits a playmate the natural outcome would be to say that if she is having a hard time controlling her temper, she should play alone until she feels that she can play nicely. Please don't ever hit, slap or bite your child to show her how it feels.

If your child has trouble with her temper or if she persists in hitting, you might look at what she's watching on TV, in the movies or during video games. Many of these programs are very violent, and in some of the cartoons terribly brutal things happen and in the next frame the victim is up and running around, seemingly unhurt.

Karin Ireland

Focus On Who Your Child Is Instead of Who He Isn't.

A child who feels that he's valued for who he is and for what he's able to do will be confident enough to take on challenges even if he doesn't know whether or not he'll succeed. One way to help your child feel valued is to focus on the things he does right more than on the things he does wrong. Chances are good he already knows his weaknesses.

If he feels approval is based on performance he might be afraid to try new things, fearing that he might fail and lose that approval.

Appreciate your child and let him know you do, not only for his successes but also for his effort and enthusiasm when he tries.

Be Willing to Admit When You're Wrong.

Young children love it when Mom or Dad is wrong. Admitting you're wrong can send good messages to older children, too. If they know that you are wrong sometimes and that you're okay with that, they're less likely to aim critical, self-defeating messages at themselves when they're wrong.

If they see you admit when you're wrong it will help them be able to admit it when they're wrong, too.

Take Advantage of Time-outs.

I t's possible to be a little nicer, a little more patient than you feel . . . but only a little. When you're already stressed and your child is adding more stress, ask for a time-out.

Talk to your child about time-outs when you aren't stressed and ask what she thinks a time-out should mean. Does she need to go to her room? Should she be able to stay in the same room as you if she doesn't talk to you? Can she go outside? Can she watch TV?

Talk about how long a time-out can be—ten or fifteen minutes? How will she know when it's finished?

Talk about how *she* might use time-outs, too. Can she use

them with you if she's feeling stressed herself? Can she use it with friends when they argue? Can she use it when a friend tries to push her into saying or doing something she doesn't want to say or do?

Karin Ireland

Divorced? You Can Make It Less Traumatic for Your Child.

D ivorce can be devastating to a child and can seriously affect his or her self-esteem. You can make it less traumatic.

Agree to keep the divorce between you and your ex. Don't make your child suffer because you and your ex can't get along.

Don't make your ex the bad guy to your child, even if he or she is. Children need to feel that both parents are valuable and that both parents love them.

Don't make your child carry angry messages to your ex. Don't punish your ex by changing or disallowing visits, "forgetting" to pass along phone messages or mail.

Make it okay for your child to write and call her other parent whenever she wants to. Make it easy for your ex to communicate with your child. Focus on the good things when you talk to your child about her other parent.

Divorced? Consider
Co-parenting.

There are books on the subject, but you can figure out a schedule that works for all of you without reading any of them.

The disadvantages of co-parenting are that it can be work and it can be confusing. The advantages are that your child gets to grow up in a close relationship with both parents.

It's helpful to live in the same neighborhood. Some children stay with each parent every other week. Some spend weekdays with one parent and weekends with the other, and some alternate so that sometimes they spend weekdays with one parent and sometimes they spend weekends.

Some children stay Sunday through Wednesday with one and Thursday through Saturday with the other. My ex and I separated when our daughter was seven (she's twenty-five now) and we alternated days: Tuesday, Thursday, and Saturday noon till Sunday noon she was with her dad and the other times she was with me. Confusing? Sometimes. But she grew up seeing each parent daily (morning or evening) and having a great relationship with both.

Good Parenting Doesn't Mean Creating a Perfect Child.

When our children are little we get into a habit of correcting many of their beliefs and actions because we know that our suggestions will help them be safe or happy or just better informed. It's a hard habit to break, but in order for a child to develop good self-esteem as she grows older, she has to know that much of the time her own way of doing things is fine.

Take time regularly to think about each of the things you're trying to get your child to do. On a scale from one to ten, how important is it, really? How important will it be to her as she grows up? What will happen if she doesn't learn the lesson or if she doesn't learn it right now? Are there any signs that she is feeling less confident, less competent because of your coaching? What lessons might you be willing to put off for another time?

Be philosophical. Our parents weren't able to make us perfect and yet we turned out fine.

Teach Your Child How to
Resolve Conflicts.

One of the keys to resolving conflicts is a good attitude, and a good attitude comes from knowing that conflicts are normal. Our parents may have taught us that conflict was bad and that it should be avoided at all costs, but now we realize that the costs are too great. There are so many differing but valid opinions these days that avoiding conflict isn't healthy even if it is possible.

Explain to your child that one of the first steps in resolving a conflict is to really understand what the conflict is. Maybe he and a friend have the same goal but don't agree on how to accomplish it. Maybe they have two different goals. Careful listening is important. Once they agree on a result both are willing to accept, they can look for ways to reach it.

Karin Ireland

Sometimes conflict is unintentional and can be resolved just by someone's letting the other person know how he feels. The friend is not likely to know unless your child speaks up, though.

Sometimes your child and a friend may decide that they can't resolve the conflict and they each need to do what they want to alone. Sometimes they'll listen and understand each other and decide they can't agree but can put the conflict behind them and stay friends.

Honor Your Promises.

Think carefully when your child asks you to promise something. Is it really something you can promise to do? Is it something you want to promise? If it isn't, be honest and say so.

If you do make a promise, be sure to keep it. If you agree to do something on a special date, write yourself a note and put it on your calendar. If you promise to do something "soon," write yourself a note and put it in your calendar. If you promise to do something in a few minutes, give up your hope of "getting everything done first" and do it in a few minutes.

When you honor your promises your child feels like he's important, like he's worth your time and attention. He gets the message that he can count on you to do what you say you'll do. He also gets a good lesson in honoring promises himself.

Karin Ireland

Set Your Child Up for Success.

C ommunication is an important part of success, and telling your child what you want her to do is only one part of communicating. When you give her instructions, make sure she actually *understands* what you want her to do, the result you want and when you want her to be finished. Give her a chance to offer feedback and ask questions.

Establish a regular study time and quiet place for her to do her schoolwork. Create an evening routine where she lays out everything she needs to take to school. Insist she eat a nutritious breakfast and not one with lots of sugar. Expect that she will be successful most of the time.

Show Your Child She's Important to You.

C hildren thrive when they know they're important to the people they love. When she asks a question, answer. Look at her; encourage her to ask more questions. Ask her opinion about things that will involve her. Value her likes and dislikes. Be respectful of her in front of her friends.

Encourage her to develop interests, even if they're different from yours. Be interested in the things that interest her. Believe her before you believe a stranger, a neighbor or even a teacher. Look for opportunities to spend time with her. Laugh at her jokes. Tell her often how much you like and love her. Save her best art-work and once in a while spend some time together admiring it.

Don't Use Guilt to Control Your Child.

G uilt is not a good way to encourage your child to do what you want him to. In addition to being hard on his self-esteem, it sets up a pattern of behavior that others can take advantage of, too. If you make him feel guilty for not doing what you want him to do, he will give in to peers when they try to make him feel guilty for not doing what *they* want him to.

Don't Let Your Child Use Guilt to Control You.

E very parent wants to be the best parent he can be, and it's easy to feel guilty if you feel you aren't doing everything you could. Most children are experts at sensing ways they can make you feel guilty and at pushing the right buttons in the hope you'll give in. Once you do, they'll be encouraged to resort to guilt the next time, and the next.

Try to remember that there isn't a parent alive who does everything right, who gives everything he can, who is as fair as she could be, who couldn't be more patient, generous or forgiving. But parents should not override their better judgment in order to keep peace with their child.

If your child does try to manipulate you with guilt, make sure that she isn't learning how by watching *you* try to manipulate *her* that way. Let her know that guilt trips won't work with you and then show her you mean it by not giving in. Once she realizes that they won't get her what she wants, she'll try them less often.

Listen for the Difference Between Guidance and Criticism.

O ften the difference between guidance and criticism can be found in one's choice of words and tone of voice. Think about how you'd respond if your boss criticized you for your shortcomings and how much more positively you'd respond if she would guide you to improve.

Take Time to Play with Your Child.

Many parents *intend* to play with their child, but first they have to . . . (fill in the blank). And when that is done they realize they really need to . . . (fill in the blank).

In our society we've pushed play deep into the "last priority" category and, as author Wayne Dyer says, forgotten that we're human beings, not human doings.

Join your child in flying a kite, bouncing or throwing a ball or blowing bubbles in the backyard. Grab a handful of Play-Doh (even if both of you are too old) and see what you can create. Skip through the park, swing on the swings and ride the merry-go-round together.

Don't put off having fun until he forgets how much fun you can be.

Help Your Child Learn to Cope with Setbacks.

S ometimes, in spite of her best efforts, your child won't meet all her goals, and it's important for her to remember that Edison tried more than a hundred ways to invent the lightbulb before he found one that actually worked! He was probably pretty good at coping with setbacks.

You can set a good example by letting your child see the positive ways you cope with setbacks. Help her understand that there will be times when her efforts will be instantly successful and other times when they won't. Show her how, instead of becoming angry or discouraged, she can evaluate the situation: What is her goal, what did she do to reach it, why did that fail, what might she do that *could* work?

Karin Ireland

Remind Your Child Often of His Past Successes.

You probably spend a part of every day thinking about the past, and as long as you're there, remember one of your child's successes. Who wouldn't feel great to hear someone say, "I was just thinking, remember what a great job you did on your science project?" or "Remember the time you won the spelling competition in your classroom?" or "Remember how much help you were to your dad when the fence blew down?"

Encourage Independence.

S ome children rush to independence, while others act as if they'd like to stay in the nest till they're adults. Appropriate independence boosts self-esteem. Here are some ways she can practice:

1. Is she able to successfully complete homework assignments without you monitoring them?

2. Is she able to communicate clearly enough to call stores to inquire if they have a special item she's looking for?

3. Can she pack her own bag for an overnight stay with a friend?

Karin Ireland

4. Can she choose the clothes she wants to wear? (Offer hints about matching if you need to, but try to keep them just hints.)

5. Can she fix some of her own meals?

Ask for Your Child's Help in Solving His Behavior Problems.

I f you've asked your child to change a behavior, have reasoned, threatened, bargained, used reverse psychology and everything else you can think of and nothing has worked, why not ask your child for advice. Say, "I'm stumped. How can we resolve this?"

Prepare yourself for him to say that one way is for you to stop asking. Don't think of this as a smart-aleck answer, because he's right—it is one way. But it's probably not a way you're comfortable with or you'd have already stopped asking. So what's another way?

Because you brought him onto the decision-making team, he may come up with an idea that could work for both of you. If he feels like he has some input, he may be willing to offer a compromise that he would have rejected if it had been your idea.

Don't Slap, Shake or Spank Your Child.

According to an article in the *Archives of Pediatrics and Adolescent Medicine,* a recent study has found that the more children from the ages of six to nine are spanked, the greater is the incidence of their being found cheating, lying and bullying.

Too often, spanking is a physical release for a frustrated adult and teaches a child that the way to deal with frustration is to hit. Stubborn children will only become more stubborn when spanked. They lose trust for the adult who is spanking them. They lose respect for themselves, too.

A child who's being spanked is not thinking that he should change his ways—he's vowing to not get caught next time; he's having ugly thoughts about the person who's hurting him, one of the people he needs to be able to trust.

Unfortunately, spanking is habit-forming, and it escalates. Each time it's easier to use more force. When spanking is being inflicted by a frustrated adult, the more frustrated he is, the more force he's likely to use. Too many children are injured every day by adults who didn't mean to go out of control—they just did. And please, never shake a child—it can result in brain damage.

If there's an adult in your child's life who believes spanking is a necessary part of discipline ask him (or her) to put himself in the child's shoes. Ask what would be going through his mind if he were forced to stand still while someone twice his size hit him?

Children who are victims of physical abuse lose a sense of trust, because it's difficult to trust someone who hits you. They lose self-esteem, because they get the message that they aren't acceptable, aren't worthy of respectful treatment.

Find Alternatives to Physical Punishment.

If you find yourself moved to slap or hit your child, try to understand why he makes you so angry. Are you trying to control him? Look for ways you can guide rather than control him. Does he resist doing something your way? Ask yourself if your way is truly the only way.

Look for ways to resolve small conflicts while they're still small.

When you feel the urge to strike your child, walk away. That takes a lot of self-control, but if you're asking your child to demonstrate self control you should be able to set a good example. You can address the situation when you're calmer.

Put yourself in your child's shoes. What would it feel like to be small and vulnerable and have someone twice your size threatening to hurt you?

Go for a fast walk. Walking can relieve some of the tension that has built up. Go for a drive, roll up the windows and yell—as loud as you can.

Enroll in a martial arts class where you're rewarded for punching and kicking—it's a great way to redirect aggressive physical energy.

Adults teach children more with their behavior than with their words.

If you know an adult who would like to change but isn't sure he can, suggest joining a support group or signing up for counseling.

Eliminate Teasing, Labeling and Practical Jokes That Hurt.

T easing may be fun, but notice if it gets out of hand. Some teasing is a sign of affection and some teasing is a release of anger. If teasing has a barb to it, the recipient won't think it's funny and it should be stopped.

Humor or practical jokes that makes your child feel uncomfortable or like the victim of an attack should be stopped. If others say, "Oh, but I was just teasing," let them know that it's not a kind thing to do and that you won't tolerate it in your home.

Labeling, even positive labels, can have bad results because it can encourage your child to act like the person she's being compared with instead of being happy being who she is.

Look for Reasons to Praise Your Child.

C hildren love to feel competent and they bask in approval. Every day, look for ways to give your child honest praise. For example:

◙ Thank you for remembering to set the table/take out the trash/wash your hands/feed the dog without my reminding you.

◙ You did a great job doing the dishes/sweeping the porch/dusting the table. Thank you.

◙ I love to see you playing so nicely with your brother/being so gentle with the cat/being such a good friend to Jamie.

Karin Ireland

◼ I really appreciate your doing your homework before you played/telling me you broke a dish/offering to rake the leaves.

Replace "Almost" Compliments with 100-Percenters.

Maybe you've had a boss or parent who said things that were *almost* a compliment, things like, "That's great you got a 95 on your paper; if you try a little harder you can get 100." Or, "That's great you got a second place in the competition—with a little more effort you can take first next time." Or, "That was a great report, but next time try to . . ."

The person means to motivate you to achieve more, but often these kinds of "almost" compliments make you feel deflated because you're not being acknowledged for the work you did do.

Avoid sending this kind of message to your child. Getting a 95 and feeling great about it does more for his self-esteem than struggling to get 100 because that's the only way he can please you.

Help Your Child Develop a Good Memory.

A good memory is an important asset in our culture, and yet no one teaches memory skills! Young children have an excellent memory—consider all that they learn. As they get older, however, their memory seems less powerful. But a good memory can be reclaimed.

When you're riding in the car, turn off the radio and practice. Make a game of asking your child to remember the order of things she's done since breakfast or lunch. Ask her to describe the placement of furniture in your living room. Ask her to tell you about the decorations on the walls of her classroom. Take turns remembering programs you watched on TV and the basic plot or story line.

Play games like "I packed my bag . . ." If she knows the alphabet, it can actually be easier. To play, one of you starts with something you'd take on a trip, saying, "I packed my bag with an apple." The next person repeats the first item and adds one: "I packed my bag with an apple and a brush." And so on.

Notice When Actions Speak Louder Than Words.

"Yes (kindly), you may..." (gentle touch on the shoulder).

"Yes (coldly), you may..." (eye roll, head shake, the smacking *tssk* sound you make with your tongue behind your top front teeth).

These two sentences have the same three words and both give permission, but one gives a message of approval and the other a clear message of disapproval. While the message of disapproval may be about the activity, the child will surely take it to mean disapproval of him, too.

Notice times when your actions may send a message that attacks his feeling of self-worth and ask yourself if there's another way for you to get your point across, kindly.

De-stress Before You Get Home.

After a hard day at work you may be longing for some peace and quiet, some time to relax. But your child may greet you enthusiastically and want to tell you all her news of the day. There goes your peace-and-quiet time.

Why not stop along the way home to de-stress? Find a quiet tree-lined street or a park or a sunny bench someplace that feels peaceful. Give yourself fifteen or twenty minutes to breathe deeply, to relax your muscles and to think pleasant thoughts.

After you've relaxed, you'll be ready to greet your child with the same level of enthusiasm with which she greets you.

Karin Ireland

Teach Your Child Appropriate Ways to Express Anger.

No one likes to be on the receiving end of anger, and so when a child is mad we often send the message that anger is bad and that expressing it is even worse. But today's health experts tell us that anger that is kept inside has to come out somehow, and often does in unhealthy ways.

Let your child know that it's okay to be angry and then help him learn to express anger in positive ways. How? One way is to set a good example. If you holler at people and things when you're upset, he'll learn from your example regardless of what you tell him he *should* do.

Encourage him to speak up when he's angry, to *talk* about the reason he's angry instead of keeping it inside or yelling and losing control. Show him how by letting him see you do it.

If he's angry with you, try listening to what he has to say. Often, just feeling he's been heard will make some of the anger go away. Be sure to let him get it all out and make sure you understand what he's saying before you try to argue or explain.

Help him learn how to find solutions to the things that make him angry. Can he let go of his expectations that other people will behave in a certain way? Can he let go of his expectations that his efforts will be successful the first time?

If his anger needs a physical release, encourage him to pound a pillow. If he has long-term anger, suggest a martial arts class, where he'll be directing all that energy into a positive exercise.

Teens Need Your Time, Too.

There's no doubt about it—teens want to be independent. But at the same time, they want to feel secure being independent. They may seem as if they're happy to be on their own most of the time, but they still need to know that they can come to you when they need to, that you like, respect and love them.

Look for events you can share together. Try to be flexible enough with your to-do schedule so that you seem approachable. When she seems like she wants to talk, stop what you're doing if you can and just listen.

Teach Him How to Plan and Complete a Project.

Successful projects take planning, and most children don't understand the steps that are involved. They're likely to believe a project will be easier than it actually will be and they'll put it off until it's too late to do a good job.

Encourage your child to tell you as soon as he finds out he has a school project to work on. Sit down with a calendar and have him count the days till the project is due. Ask him to write down the steps he plans to take to complete the project and what days he plans to take them. Show him how to build in a few days for emergencies.

Once he's completed a reasonable schedule, ask him to make a copy for you, and for the first few projects monitor his progress.

Teach Your Child to Be Comfortable with Change.

The world our children are growing up in changes almost every day. It seems that few things can be counted on to last forever and that tomorrow something we never dreamed possible may be commonplace.

Today's kids need to be flexible, need to understand that it's good to have a plan, a goal, but at the same time they need to be flexible enough to accept and even benefit from change.

How can you help your child learn to be comfortable with change? One way is to practice being flexible yourself. Another is to look at the way you live as a family. If everything is always planned out in advance, if you go through with all plans no matter what, your child could become so comfortable with routines that she's uncomfortable when they're altered.

Look for ways to add variety to what you do and when you do it. Help him look at new things as an adventure instead of a risk.

Encourage Your Child to Read.

R eading has never been more important to a person's success than it is now. Computers and even the Internet are already a part of many schools and students must be able to read fairly well to be able to navigate the instructions, let alone cope with the staggering amount of information a good search can find.

Make reading fun! Read to him, read with him, encourage him to read to you. Let him see you enjoy reading. Look for books that explore subjects he already has an interest in. Help him find books in the library that he likes to read, even if you don't think they're educational.

Ask him to read signs, directions and instructions to you. Send him postcards or letters in the mail. Let him keep the lights on half an hour past bedtime and read. Of course, he'll ask if he can play instead, but keep this a time just for reading. Make sure he's all ready for bed and that he takes a stack of books with him—if he gets out of bed to get more books he might be distracted by a toy.

Teach Your Child How to Manage Money.

Money management was simple before borrowing (by way of credit cards and bank checks) became so easy. The basic rule is still a good one: Don't spend money until you have it.

Teach your child that it's impossible for most people to have everything they want and so it's important to learn how to choose. Encourage her to make a list of things she'd like to have and the approximate cost. When she saves enough for the lowest-priced item on her list, she can decide to buy it or to put the money toward something else.

If she looks at her list every few days, she'll probably notice that some things start to seem less important. She can cross these off her list. Chances are that if she had bought them, she would have soon lost interest and her money would be gone!

Ask Lots of "What Would You Do If . . ." Questions.

When a child feels he knows what to do it boosts his self-esteem. By asking lots of "What if" questions you can help your child think about situations and help him be capable. Ask, "What would you do if someone tried to get you to go into a car with them? What would you do if you were home alone and there was a fire? What would you do if someone offered you something that looked like medicine? What would you do if you were home alone during an earthquake?"

Those are some of the scarier things that can happen to a child, but it's good to ask simpler questions, too. Things like, "What would you do if your teacher said you did something you didn't do? What would you do if you saw someone in the playground hurting someone else? What would you do if somebody offered to help you cheat on a test? What would you do if you found some money and a friend said you should just keep it?"

Since this is a thinking process, don't expect all the first answers to be perfect.

Encourage Your Child to Discover Her Own Solutions.

T here's a quote that says, "Teach your child how to think, not what to think," and you do that when you encourage her to discover her own solutions. When she comes to you with a question, ask her sometimes what *she* thinks the answer might be. If she says she doesn't know, ask questions to help her start thinking in the right direction.

Save Great Schoolwork.

Have a drawer or a box where you can put samples of great schoolwork. Then every few months sit down together and go through the collection and be amazed all over again at what a great job he did.

Teach Your Child to Recognize What Stresses Her and to Do Something About It.

P arents think kids live stress-free lives because they believe they have few of the pressures adults have. That may be true, but children have stress that comes from teachers, homework, tests, friends . . . and parents.

Encourage her to recognize how she feels when she's stressed. Maybe she already knows when she's stressed but doesn't know she can do anything about it. Help her see if some of the things that stress her can be eliminated. Can she see less of that friend who isn't really very nice to her? Can she eliminate some of her after-school activities if she's feeling overwhelmed? Can she stop trying to be a perfect pianist and enjoy playing at whatever level she does?

Encourage her to eat healthy food, drink lots of water and get plenty of sleep. Suggest that she participate in an activity that puts her stress energy to good use—school sports, martial arts, dancing, jogging.

Get her a simple book on meditation and encourage her to take time every day to practice. Give her a pretty journal and encourage her to write out her feelings, and promise her you'll never look.

Try to Correct Your Child in Private.

Being corrected generally isn't that pleasant, but it's even less pleasant if a friend overhears. When you need to correct your child, try to do it in a positive way, and try to do it in private.

Sometimes Do Less *for* Your Child and More *with* Him.

I t's easy to fall into a pattern of doing so much for your child that you don't have much time to *be* with him. Try not to get caught up working long hours so that you have money to buy him things. Most of the time he'll benefit more from your time than from your gifts. Your time is an important way to tell him you like and value him.

Don't sign him up for so many after-school activities that all your time together is spent with you watching him from afar! Look for activities you can do together, and leave time to do nothing together, too.

Let Your Child Know It's Okay Not to Be Perfect.

A child may get the idea at home that she needs to be perfect, and when she goes to school the message is even stronger. As a result, she may feel like a failure when she doesn't get the highest grade, when she isn't the best on her sports team, when she doesn't live up to other people's expectations of her. At some point she may give up trying hard, and maybe she won't try at all.

Let her know that no one can be perfect and that what you want is for her to do her best.

Applaud her enthusiasm and effort as well as their results. If schoolwork needs to improve, look for ways to help her without expecting her to be perfect.

Look for Ways to Show Your Child You Love Him.

Someone who knows he's truly loved, not just when he's good but even when he's awful, is blessed. The more ways you can show your child you love him, the more he will know you do.

Treat him the way you'd treat a valued friend. Treat him the way you'd like to have him treat you. Appreciate his enthusiasm. Let him hear about the ways you admire him. Speak kindly. Tell him you love him. Hug and kiss him as long as he'll let you.

Karin Ireland

Teach Your Child to Trust Her Perceptions.

Teaching your child to trust her perceptions will help her learn to make wise decisions about people and situations. She'll develop a sensing device to help her determine if someone is telling the truth, whether someone is in reality too busy to do what she says she'll do, if a group will work well together or not and even whether or not a place is safe.

You can help teach your child to trust her perceptions by being honest with her about your feelings. If she thinks you're angry and you are, admit it instead of saying you aren't.

It's natural to try to act brave when you're sad or hurt, but let her know you're trying to act brave instead of attempting to convince her that you don't feel the feeling.

Teach Your Child to Feel and Trust His Feelings.

Many of us were taught as children to ignore our feelings, and we may be passing the same messages on to our children. "Shush, don't cry, it's not that bad." "How can you say you don't like Jimmy when he was so nice to you last week?" "I'm sure Mary isn't really mad at you. . . ."

It's alarming how easily these messages come. Sometimes we're trying to comfort a child, to make the pain go away; sometimes we're trying to comfort ourselves, to make the pain go away; sometimes we're trying to teach a child to balance the good with the bad.

What we're really saying, though, is "You may think something is painful but a) you're wrong or b) it's not okay to admit it."

Feelings aren't right or wrong, they just are! And if they aren't

Karin Ireland

acknowledged, if they get stuffed inside, they come out at another time in another (often inappropriate) way.

Instead of telling your child how he "should" feel, encourage him to talk about the hurt. Let him know that it's okay to feel what he feels and that he can express his feelings to you.

Being able to feel his feelings of anger, pain, frustration and fear will help him be able to let those feelings go.

Learning to trust his feelings will help him make decisions about who to trust and what kinds of activities will be safe and fun.

Encourage Your Child to Set
Personal Boundaries.

S etting boundaries is one of the ways we protect ourselves from the outside world. Our boundaries tell
others it's okay to do this but not that . . . I will do these things
for you but not those.

Your child may start setting boundaries with her family by
asking you not to call her by a certain nickname, not to hug her
in public or not to tell others about something embarrassing that
happened to her.

Your respecting her boundaries tells your child she is valuable, that she is worthy of respect, that she deserves to have her
needs met.

In addition to the boundaries she asks you to respect, here
are some that are traditional. Knock before you go into your

child's room. Don't open mail addressed to her, don't share her secrets with others, don't tease in hurtful ways, don't look in drawers and don't read her journal.

Encourage her to set boundaries with her friends, too. Let her know it's okay to say no when they want her to do something she doesn't want to do.

Help Your Child Evaluate Fear Instead of Stuffing It Inside or Backing Away.

A fear is a feeling based on a perception. Some fears are helpful, and even lifesaving—for example, the fear of running out into traffic. But being afraid of safe situations, being afraid to try new things can keep your child from discovering people and activities he might really enjoy.

Sometimes it's tempting for a frustrated parent to try to get his child to face a fear by pushing him, by ridiculing him for being afraid or by minimizing his fears. What can happen, though, is that the child may argue in defense of his fears, thus reinforcing them, or that he'll bury them inside and pretend he doesn't care.

Help your child evaluate his fears by asking questions like: When was the first time he remembers feeling that fear? Has something like that ever actually happened to him? To anyone he knows? What does he think might be the worst thing that could happen? How would he deal with the situation if it did?

Learn to recognize the difference between a concern, in which case he may want your assurance that it's really no big deal, and a serious fear, where nothing you can say will make it go away. Let him know it's safe to talk to you by listening without rushing to try to make him feel better.

Ask Your Child for His Opinion.

K ids love to think they have all the answers, and it's a boost to their self-esteem when people they care about ask for advice. But there's another reason to ask: Kids can give great advice. After all, they haven't yet learned all the reasons something can't be done.

Tell Your Child the Story, "The Day You Were Born..."

Of course, Mom had a big part to play that day, but your child will love to hear about the day he was the center of everyone's attention and about how cute he was, how loved he is, how happy everyone is that he is part of your family.

Take out the family photo album and look at the pictures. Talk about your memories of each event.

Anything Worth Doing Is Worth Doing Poorly . . . at First.

V ery young children are willing to try all kinds of activities, because they don't worry about "failing." But at some point they get the message that success brings approval and failure brings disapproval, and many decide to play it safe from then on.

While some people do seem to learn everything instantly and perfectly, most don't. Ask anyone who is great how she got that way and she'll say, "By practice."

Help your child understand that success is often the result of lots of practice, lots of not being successful at first. And that anything worth doing is worth doing poorly until he has enough experience to begin to do it well.

Karin Ireland

If at First You Don't Succeed . . . Maybe Try Something Else.

The original version of this was "If at first you don't succeed, try, try again." And certainly persistence is important and many activities do require repeated efforts in order for one to succeed at them.

But things change so quickly today, and there are so many options, that plugging along doggedly is not the guarantee of success it once was. Someone who can do her best and be willing to change directions if necessary is more likely to succeed than someone who keeps trying to do the same thing the very same way. There's truth to the saying, "If you keep doing what you're doing, you'll keep getting what you're getting."

Help your child learn when to push for what she wants and when to change direction. Some activities may just not be right for your child, or the approach she is taking may not work for her. Instead of watching her continue to try the same thing the same way and failing again and again, help her look at what she's trying to accomplish. Does she really want or need to accomplish that goal? If the answer is yes, what are five other ways she might accomplish it? (By thinking until she comes up with five possibilities, she's more likely to devise one that will actually work.)

If she decides she doesn't really want or need to accomplish that goal, maybe it's time to choose a new one and to work toward that.

Help your child learn how much time and energy she should spend trying to accomplish a result before deciding to look at another option. Let her see you change your goals sometimes and let her know how and why you decided to. Talk to her about your new goal.

Understand Where Your Parenting Rules Come From.

E veryone expects that when we have a child we'll automatically know how to be a parent. All we know automatically, though, is how our parents parented.

Notice the ways you parent as your parents did. Then notice if your child is happy, flourishing, if he has good self-esteem. If he does, keep it up! If he doesn't, look for rules, attitudes or expectations you have that don't seem to be working with him.

Once parents were expected to be authoritarian, to force a child into an accepted role, and now we know that a child will be more successful if the parent guides rather than forces him in the right direction. Blind obedience was once considered a good thing, and now we recognize it as dangerous—a child needs to be independent enough to say no to peer pressure.

Keep Your Expectations Reasonable.

When children are very young it's easy not to have great expectations. Their limitations are obvious and we accept them. As they get older, they start seeming more competent and we expect more. Sometimes we expect more than they're able to deliver and we get frustrated. Of course, they're frustrated, too.

On the other hand, not expecting enough from your child can send messages to her that you don't think she's capable of doing very much.

Somewhere in the middle are expectations that are appropriate—ones that she can reasonably be expected to meet. Take time to really look at her, and notice her strengths and weaknesses. Try to help her build skills and confidence in areas where she is weak. Encourage her to reach a little, but not so much that success seems impossible. Expect miracles and then be happy with what you get.

Talk with Your Child About Your Expectations.

You might think your child is successful because he's willing to try new challenges and to throw himself into experiences. He may think you measure success only by the result. You might value honesty, kindness and integrity and your child may think you'd rather have a sports jock or a math whiz. The result is that you might think he's quite successful and he may feel like a failure, unless he knows how you measure success.

Talk with your child about your expectations, and invite him to talk about his, too.

Play Games That Boost Self-Esteem.

C hildren love to play games, and here are some that will help increase self-esteem.

One is to choose a stuffed animal and toss it back and forth to each other. As the first person tosses, she says something positive to the receiver, like. "I think it's wonderful that you remember to feed the dog." The other then tosses the animal back and might say, "I love your cooking." Keep this up until both of you feel great.

Or play "Inside/outside." Take turns saying something about the person inside ("You're honest") and outside ("You have a great smile"). Or try the "Three things" game—"Three things I like about you are . . . ," followed by "Three things I like about me are . . ."

Here's a game you can play while driving in the car: Take turns saying why you're happy to be the other's parent or child.

These are fun ways to remind your child of all the ways she's special—and you get to remember ways you're special, too!

Occasionally Change the Filter Through Which You See Your Child.

Every once in a while, look at your child with new eyes. Have you been thinking of him as the young boy he was last year? Are you remembering him as a klutz even though he isn't any longer? Do you think of him as lazy even though he's actually been quite a lot of help lately?

Pretend you are him right now and imagine what he might like to tell you about the boy he is today. What old ideas can you let go of? What new things can you compliment him on?

Avoid These Messages That Lower Self-Esteem.

■ Body language (posture, gestures, facial expressions) that shows you are disappointed, exasperated, disapproving, uninterested or in any other way withholding approval.

■ Comments: Who do you think you are? What makes you think you're so special? Why do you always/never (fill in the blank)?

■ Labels (shorty, klutzy, late bloomer, the slow one, lazybones).

■ Indifference toward him when he wants your attention.

Try Not to Pass Along Your Fear to Your Children.

Y ou're probably already careful not to pass along fears of things like spiders and snakes, but there are other fears you may not realize your child can inherit. For example:

1. There is never enough money for all our needs.

2. Most people are not honest.

3. Most people will take advantage of me if I'm not always alert.

4. If I don't struggle, I won't succeed.

5. People "like us" don't have what it takes to succeed.

If these are fears someone in your family has, chances are good your child is getting the message. Try to avoid saying things that reinforce these beliefs and, if it helps, use affirmations to change your thinking.

Respect Your Child's Opinions Even When You Don't Agree.

Before the era of "enlightened parenting," only one opinion was allowed in the house, and it was invariably a parent's. Fortunately, these days we know that two or more people can hold different yet valid opinions. This is an important message for kids to understand, and you can teach it by listening to and respecting your child's opinions even when you don't agree.

Showing that you value her even though you disagree is a great boost to her self-esteem. Sometimes when you don't agree, encourage her to try to use facts and logic to persuade you to change your mind—this can help her build critical thinking and communication skills.

Let Your Child Experience the Consequences of His Behavior.

I t's natural to want to take care of your child, to want to fix his mistakes so he doesn't have to be unhappy, and it's kind to do that some of the time because when you help him, you teach him to help others.

But he does need to learn that there are consequences to all of his actions and that some of them are negative. If he breaks a window and you pay to have it fixed because you feel sorry for him, he may think that he doesn't need to be careful, since you'll always be there to fix his mistakes. But if he has to pay for the window, or do extra chores to help pay for it, he'll be learning that he needs to be responsible for his behavior.

As he gets older the decisions he makes can have more serious outcomes, and it's important for him to get in the habit of thinking about the results of his behavior before he acts.

Karin Ireland

Teach Your Child About
Personal Integrity.

When we think of integrity we think of having high morals, of choosing to do what's honest and fair. There's another kind of integrity, though, and people with high self-esteem have it. The other kind is personal integrity, and it means doing what's right for *yourself*.

When your child is acting in integrity with herself, she can say no to a friend who asks to borrow something your child really doesn't want to loan. She can say no if her friend asks for a favor she doesn't want to do.

This doesn't mean she shouldn't look for ways to compromise. But compromising comes into play when someone willingly agrees to do something. When a person gives in unwillingly because she's been taught to be nice to everyone but herself, she's not acting with personal integrity. And haven't you noticed that when you let someone push you it leads to resentment, which in turn eventually leads to anger? Or you let someone push you, someone ends up in trouble and you say, "I *knew* I should have said no!"

Don't Always Minimize Your Child's Troubles and Fears. Don't "Disasterize" Them, Either.

Often we brush aside our child's troubles and fears with the best of intentions. We think that if we make light of them, somehow they will *be* lighter. Sometimes that's true, but often it isn't.

If we always minimize our children's troubles and fears, it sends the message that we don't understand what they're experiencing, that we're not willing to take them seriously enough to recognize what they are feeling. Often the wisest path is to let them talk and to nod or "hmmm" at appropriate times.

Sometimes we slip into the habit of warning our child about every negative possibility. We do this with the best of intentions, too. We believe that if we warn them about all the bad things that can happen, we're giving them the information they'll need to make sure they don't. But this can send the message that we expect them to fail.

Often the wisest path is to cross your fingers and hope for the best.

Encourage Your Child
to Be Himself.

O kay, so you've always wanted a doctor or lawyer in the family, or you love sports and know your son could be an all-star someday if he'd just try a little harder. . . . Unfortunately, that may be your dream, but not your child's.

To have high self-esteem, a child needs to know he's accepted by his parents and family for who he is, not for how close he can come to who they want him to be.

If he has a passion for sports, he'll be happier playing soccer even though you'd rather he were fascinated with computers like you are. Or he might be a computer whiz while you'd rather he be more athletic.

Give him an opportunity to experience a lot of activities, then support him in the ones he chooses.

Send "You Are Special" Messages to Your Child Regularly.

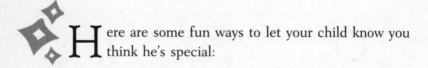Here are some fun ways to let your child know you think he's special:

- Tape a page of notebook paper to the refrigerator and every day write down one way you think he's special. When the page is full, put it in a notebook folder to look through on a rainy day.

- Hide "You are special because . . ." notes in the pages of his schoolbooks.

- Tuck a note under his pillow or crumple one at the foot of his bed where he'll feel it with his toes.

- Slip a note into his backpack, lunch box or sock drawer.

Karin Ireland

- Buy one very special plate (look in a nice thrift store) and save it for occasions when you want to tell him you think he's extra special.

- Send him a "Special friend" or congratulations card in the mail.

- Leave a message for him on the answering machine when you know he'll pick it up.

- Create a secret "I think you're special" sign to use in crowds or other places where you can't say it out loud.

- Invite him to do an errand with you and surprise him by making the errand something fun—like going for ice cream.

- Go to his sporting and school events, and go enthusiastically.

Let Your Child Know You Love Her, No Matter What.

Even though your child loves you no matter what you do, it takes a while for her to realize that you love her unconditionally, too.

There are several things you can do to help her understand. When she does something wrong, try to focus on what she did or didn't do without sounding critical of her for who she is.

Explain (repeatedly if you need to) that even though you don't always like what she does, you'll always love her. Let her *feel* that you love her, too.

There are several fun "Would you still love me if . . ." types of books for young children, and you can make a game out of it, too. Take turns asking each other "Would you still love me if . . ." questions.

Don't Expect Your Child
to Learn Every Lesson
the First Time.

He seems so wise, so grown-up. You expect to be able to tell him something once and have him a) get it, b) accept it, c) remember it and d) do it! Not just once but from now on. Good luck.

Even though we feel we know our child inside and out, the truth is that we don't really know how he thinks. We don't know how much of each message he understands, how much he accepts, or how much he cares about it. And whether he learns the lesson the first time or the fiftieth will depend on those things.

Be patient at first. Look for ways to make learning easy, interesting and rewarding. If it seems like you've turned into a nag, ask yourself if this lesson is really an important one for your child to learn. If it is, at some point he will need to take responsibility for the lesson himself. A child's self-esteem will suffer if he's expected to be better than he can possibly be, but it will also suffer if he never learns to be responsible for his own behavior.

Karin Ireland

Fifty Messages That Boost Self-Esteem.

1. I love you.

2. Keep up the good work.

3. You did a great job.

4. Thank you for . . .

5. You're a great kid.

6. I'm glad you're my son/daughter.

7. You're one of my favorite people.

8. What would I do without you?

9. Thank you for doing that with me.

10. You can do it.

11. I believe in you.

12. You're fun to be with.

13. Excellent!

14. I admire the way you did that.

15. You're so clever.

16. I really appreciate you.

17. Thanks for your help.

18. You figured that out nicely.

19. Good job on that paper.

20. You look nice.

21. Keep up the good work.

22. I always know you can figure things out.

23. I trust you.

24. You're one of the best (fill in the blank) I know.

25. I admire you for the work you do on your school assignments.

26. I really appreciate your help.

Karin Ireland

27. I love having you as my son/daughter.

28. I really like spending time with you.

29. I know you can do it.

30. You did a great job again.

31. You were really brave to do that.

32. I like the way you handled that situation.

33. You can do whatever you set your mind to.

34. Congratulations!

35. You've really gotten good at . . .

36. You're really special.

37. You have great ideas.

38. I admire your patience.

39. I'm amazed at how quickly you figured that out.

40. Thank you for remembering . . .

41. You're right.

42. I never thought of it that way.

43. Your friends are lucky to have you.

44. I heard a compliment about you today . . .

45. You're so good at math (art, drama, etc.).

46. I'm really proud of you.

47. You're terrific.

48. I trust your judgment about that.

49. I love your sense of humor.

50. You really contribute a lot to this family.